Bygone Arbroath
John Alexander

This little van was evidently the pride and joy of the West Port Association, a local co-operative society founded in 1834. It offered best quality at low prices and clean handling of goods by courteous staff.

© John Alexander, 2022
First published in the United Kingdom, 2022,
by Stenlake Publishing Ltd.
www.stenlake.co.uk
ISBN 978-1-84033-944-4

The publishers regret that they cannot supply copies of any pictures featured in this book.

Printed by
Claro Print, Office 26, 27, 1 Spiersbridge Way,
Thornliebank, Glasgow G46 8NG

Further Reading

The following were the principal books and websites used by the author during his research.

Arbroath Year Book, various dates.
Brown, Rev. Thomas, *Annals of the Disruption*, 1884.
Fitzpatrick, Linda, *The Real Price of Fish*, 2010.
Gifford, John, *The Buildings of Scotland, Dundee and Angus*, 2012.
Hallewell, Richard, *Scotland's Sailing Fishermen*, 1991.
I'Anson, Mark, *Scotland's East Coast Fishing Industry*, 2009.
Little, Lawson, *Kerr's Minature Railway*, 2000.
MacGibbon, David and Ross, Thomas, *The Ecclesiastical Architecture of Scotland*, 1897.
Scharlau, Fiona, *Old Arbroath*, 2001.
Thomas, John and Turnock, David, *A Regional History of the Railways of Great Britain, Vol. 15, North of Scotland*, 1989.
Walker, Bruce and Ritchie, Graham, *Exploring Scotland's Heritage, Fife and Tayside*, 1987.

A number of subject specific websites were also consulted as well as general sites: Canmore, NLS Maps, British Newspaper Archive and Dictionary of Scottish Architects.

'Whiskies, brandies, rums and wines of the best vintages' were available at The Red Lion Bar at 2-4 Barngreen, and the draught and bottled beers were 'always in sparkling condition'.

Introduction

Aberbrothock, which means 'at the mouth of the Brothock Water', is the old name for Arbroath and it was given to the abbey founded in 1178 by King William I 'the Lion'. When he died in 1214, he was buried there and reinterred a short time later as building work advanced. The completed church was dedicated in 1233. After that, additions and alterations continued for some time, as did repairs to damage caused by fires and fighting. Conflict characterised these turbulent times and so, in 1320, a group of barons gathered at the abbey to draw up a 'declaration' petitioning the Pope to acknowledge the country's independence and Robert the Bruce as lawful king. Despite the historical significance of that event, the building was starved of funds after the Reformation of 1560 and fell into disrepair. Unwanted and unloved it became a quarry for building stone, and was in a sorry state when Dr Samuel Johnson visited in 1773. Impressed, he described the ruins as 'fragments of magnificence'. They had been taken into state guardianship and were receiving better care by 1951 when students, who had spirited the Stone of Destiny out of Westminster Abbey the previous year, left it in the Abbey of Aberbrothock.

The town grew up around the abbey, but with Angus at the heart of Pictish territory, an earlier settlement may have existed and there is evidence of that at St Vigeans where a number of carved stones have been found. In more modern times, a thriving town developed around some key industries, notably power loom factories making linen, and spinning mills providing the yarn. The principal products were cloth for ships' sails and brown linen named after the German town of Osnaburgh. Boots and shoes were another of the town's products, but the industry that Arbroath is more widely identified with is fishing. Development of the harbour stimulated this and other marine activities, as did the building of that great aid to navigation, the Bell Rock lighthouse, one of the marvels of Scottish civil engineering.

The arrival of railways in the 19th century improved connections with the wider world. Within the town, many shops opened up along the High Street and other town centre locations attracting people from the large rural hinterland as well as local customers. As the 20th century progressed, Arbroath set about attracting more visitors from distant places by marketing itself as a tourist destination, with a range of recreational facilities mainly sited along the West Links. More organised sports also grew and the maroon clad local football team became a fixture in the Scottish leagues.

The footballers continue to do battle, but the old industries have mainly gone and while fishing has also declined Arbroath continues to reinvent itself to meet the challenges of changing times. Heritage plays a big part; the enhanced harbour area attracts visitors, as does the abbey, the museums, Hospitalfield arts centre and the glorious coastal scenery. Eight centuries and more after King William the Lion founded his abbey, the town still thrives.

The Abbey of Aberbrothock as it was about 1910.

Street and place names in Scotland can be confusing. 'Gate', as in Seagate or Marketgate, means a street or road, while 'port' means a gate. Guthrie Port, depicted here, is therefore the gateway in and out of Arbroath to the north-west where Guthrie Castle and lands have held sway in the area for a long time. The large shop on the extreme left of the picture was a main outlet for the Arbroath Equitable Co-operative Society at a time when people rarely left their immediate locality for everyday shopping. Since then the bustle has gone and the view down the brae has changed. The old buildings in the distance, facing camera, have been cleared to make way for new ones and to allow for a revamped road layout that speeds traffic through the town.

The building on the right hand edge of the picture on the facing page is shown in full in this picture from about 1910 on the corner with Hamilton Green. It was evidently used for a hairdressing business, while the neighbouring fruit merchant, H. Ross, also had a shop in High Street. To the right, the Gothic styled Inverbrothock Free Church was built in 1888/89 to the designs of architect, John Rust. He was an Aberdonian whose work was so heavily concentrated in and around the city that this church appears to be the only building that he worked on outside Aberdeen. He was appointed to the role of city architect in 1892. Continuing into the distance, Hamilton Green merged into North Port, another of the town's early gateways.

This view shows the same section of Guthrie Port as on page 4, but from the opposite direction looking toward the buttressed wall that surrounds the abbey precincts. The most prominent feature is the corner tower, 26 feet square and 70 feet high. It is a splendid example of a defensive medieval structure, with corbels at the top to carry a parapet from which people inside the abbey could keep attackers at bay by dropping stones and other deterrent things on them – a sad commentary on a time when a structure built for peace and worship had to be configured for conflict. At the time this picture was taken, Harper's Tea Rooms opposite the abbey in Guthrie Port, exhorted customers to try their 'Celebrated Arbroath Rock', a confectionery the abbey's defenders and attackers might have preferred, to hurling real rocks at each other.

In the picture on the facing page there are a number of wooden crates sitting at the roadside, they are outside the Arbroath Equitable Co-operative Society shop shown here. The society had a number of stores around the town with branches at Fergus Street, Brothock Bridge, and Keptie Street, but its main presence was at Guthrie Port where it also had separate stores, or 'departments' for boots, clothing and the one shown here, drapery, with the staff evidently happy to pose for the camera. The Equitable was one of a number of co-ops in the town; there was the West Port Association (page 1), the High Street Co-operative Society and the Co-operative Coal Society. These retail societies eventually united as one and, after a number of name changes and store reductions, became part of the wider modern Co-op.

With the abbey at one end and the harbour at the other, High Street forms the spine of the town. Like all good streets dating from medieval times it isn't ramrod straight, but takes the occasional kink and undulates gently with the lie of the land. It is seen here looking south from the abbey precincts, on the left. The picture is undated, but could be from around the 1920s judging by the style of hats worn by the young women in the foreground. They have just walked past J. P. Gibb's Hairdressing Rooms, a butcher's shop that belonged to Andrew Ruxton and alongside that, Johnston's Grand Emporium on the corner with James Street.

Johnston's Grand Emporium was one of Arbroath's retail institutions. It occupied two shops in the town, one in Commerce Street and this one at 280 High Street. The top end of James Street is on the left. On the evidence of this picture, the emporia were well stocked with a wide range of items, especially hardware and ironmongery, china, glassware and fancy goods. They also sold inexpensive travelling trunks and bags, ladies handbags, purses and combs. Advertisements promoted each shop as 'the spot for presents' and also cleverly expanded the slogan that appears above the door in this picture to read 'The House for Everything and Everything for the House'.

The photographer who took this picture looking up High Street has artfully populated it with people who all convey a splendid period flavour. Two men with a bicycle stand in the centre of the road while to the left another two have removed some cobbles to carry out some work. On the right a young woman, possibly a nanny, has carefully positioned her up-market pram on the footpath where a young man-about-town stands outside Mrs C. W. McMullen's drapery store. The adjacent shop with the two pendant globe lights was a branch of the Maypole Dairy, while across the street the shop with many pendant lights was a branch of Boots, the chemist.

High Street is seen here in 1934 looking toward the turreted block on the corner with Kirk Square, where McMullen's drapery store was situated. To the right is a plain three-storied building that was formerly the White Hart Inn, built in 1821. At street level, the frontage has been altered to accommodate shops, with the one to the right being that of F. W. Woolworth's 3d and 6d Stores. The store, which also had an entrance from Kirk Square, opened in 1933. Popularly known as 'Woolies', Woolworth's stores were a feature of high streets around the country, but all closed around the same time. The Arbroath Woolies shut in December 2008.

In its heyday the High Street was lined with a wonderful variety of shops. There were clothing and baby linen shops, hatters, tobacconists, chemists, bakers, grocers, dairies, tea rooms, furniture warehouses, insurance offices and many more including at No. 148 the shop run by butcher and poulterer, Robert Forbes. Modern hygiene inspectors would probably have apoplexy at the sight of the rabbits, hares and pheasants hanging outside, but such displays were common when this picture was taken and used as a postcard in 1907. The striped aprons worn by the men were like a uniform for butchers and often appear in old photographs looking less than clean – that would also offend against modern standards of food safety.

The main civic buildings in the burgh were grouped together toward the southern end of High Street. They are seen on the left of this picture with the one nearest camera, with arched first floor window and projecting roof pediment, built in 1814-15 as the Trades Hall. The awning on the ground floor shades the windows of Lamb's, 'the premier butcher, poulterer and game dealer in the district'. Further up the street is the Town Hall and Sheriff Court, built in 1806-08 and the neighbouring Guildry Buildings of 1880-81. The large building on the right of the picture was erected for the Prudential Assurance Company in 1915-16, a couple of doors down from the furniture emporium of D. T. Wilson & Sons. Another prominent public building, the Webster Memorial Hall was built in the 1860s, a little further down the street behind the camera.

The Prudential Assurance building in High Street was situated on the corner with Hill Street where another of the town's key buildings, the main post office, was sited. It was evidently a much-desired addition to the town because the opening in May 1900 was described as a 'relief' for townspeople, a reference to recent events in the South African War. That didn't stop criticism being aimed at the chosen site, that it was not ideal but had been used well for the building, seen here in a postcard from 1904. Arbroath has an honoured place in postal history because a native of the town, James Chalmers, has been credited with inventing the postage stamp, three years before Rowland Hill (later Sir Rowland) was publicly credited with the invention. Although the old post office has since closed, the lower part of the building on the right has been adapted for modern usage.

Another of the town's keynote buildings, the public library, is seen here in a picture from about 1912. Originally built in 1821 as Arbroath Academy the building was redesigned to serve as the library when the school, restyled as Arbroath High School, moved to a new site off Keptie Road in the mid 1890s. As well as housing books and all the other delights of a library, the building incorporated an art gallery, in two rooms on the first floor. Highlights of the collection are two large paintings by Peter Brueghel the Younger donated to the town in the mid 19th century. This view of the building from Hill Terrace also shows Academy Street with St Mary the Virgin Episcopal Church in background, built in the 1850s with a distinctive tall steeple.

The lower end of High Street is seen in this photo looking toward the shore. Just to the right of centre is a three-storied building, which was replaced in 1915-16 by the Prudential Assurance building shown on page 13. That helps to date the picture and also the activity in the foreground, in front of the Town House. It appears to show the crowd assembled in July 1913 to witness the sale of a silver tea urn confiscated from a Miss A. J. Macgregor, proprietrix of Abbeythune House near Inverkeillor in lieu of unpaid taxes. After a few derisory offers the bidding rose to a sum well in excess of Miss Macgregor's debt, but she may have felt the loss of this family heirloom was worthwhile because it had helped to make her point for women's rights.

Following the sale of the tea urn Miss Macgregor's supporters held a protest meeting at Brothock Bridge, which this picture appears to show. The speaker, standing on a carriage, could be a Miss Grant from Dundee. She was a suffragette, a member of the Women's Social and Political Union, but the 'NO VOTE NO TAX' banner alongside her was the slogan of the Women's Tax Resistance League, the organisation that Miss Macgregor was a member of – as a property owner she would have been liable for tax, but as a woman was denied the vote and had refused to pay. She had earlier, in 1909, played host to women who had staged a hunger strike in Dundee and also held a protest meeting at Brothock Bridge.

The Brothock Water may have given Arbroath its name, but in the centre of town the Brothock Bridge largely hid it from view. The bridge also formed an open urban space, like a hub or town square, with streets radiating from it in all directions – the ideal location for band concerts and public gatherings. It is seen here in a picture from about 1920 with a crowd bustling past the range of single-storey shops on the left. Facing camera on the right is a building erected in the 1850s as a bank for the British Linen Company. Formed in 1746 the company was initially set up to encourage development of the linen industry and although it acted as a bank, was not formally permitted to use the title, British Linen Bank, until 1906.

The British Linen Bank is on the left of this picture from the late 1950s looking across Brothock Bridge to Commerce Street. The two cyclists will have been grateful that the main through route had been surfaced with tarmac, leaving triangles of cobbles for the remaining areas. To the right, the photographer has included the back end of one of Walter Alexander's buses – that flying 'bluebird' symbol was a familiar sight on roads around central and eastern Scotland. Run by baker Arthur Masson, the Stance Café beside Alexander's premises was the kind of catering establishment that no self respecting bus stance could do without. Alongside, the Arbroath Co-operative Society store was originally an Arbroath Equitable store before the local co-ops amalgamated.

Leading away from the southeast corner of Brothock Bridge and along to High Street, Commerce Street is seen here in another late 1950s picture almost certainly taken on the same day as the one on the previous page. With the British Linen Bank at the Brothock Bridge end, the Trades Hall on the corner with High Street, and the Corn Exchange, tucked in behind it, the street was well named. It was also a busy commercial thoroughfare, with one of the principal retail outlets being Henderson's Emporium in the centre of the picture, which sold a variety of products including clocks, cutlery, carpet ends and more besides. On the right, people, could inspect Morris and Wolseley cars at Law's Garage showroom, and other shops in the street sold ladies and gents clothing, fruit, vegetables and flowers, household goods, electrical appliances and gramophone records. This really was a street of commerce.

Commerce Street and Brothock Bridge also form the background to these pictures of a man known as 'Stumpie' Cuthbert. He was a fruit and vegetable merchant and, wearing a baggy suit and 'toorie bunnet', he hauled his barrow around the town selling his wares. Here he seems to be not so much selling as giving something to a white cat that has crossed his path. The reason he was called 'Stumpie' is evident in the picture on the left; he had a wooden left leg. In more modern times with social security and a state funded health service he would have been fitted with a proper prosthetic, but in the early 20th century, when these pictures were taken, he just had to 'get on with it'.

Upstream from Brothock Bridge another bridge spanned the burn connecting Bridge Street on the west bank and Panmure Street on the east. The latter is seen here looking toward the Abbey in the distance. It evidently hosted a number of small businesses including Storrier's licensed grocery and provision shop on the left and it occasionally hosted floods when the Brothock Water overflowed. An unlucky street perhaps, one of those demolished when the A92 Burnside Drive relief road was constructed in the 1960s. The need for traffic improvements was recognised in a pre- Second World War by-pass scheme but that was deemed too expensive after the war leaving the town council with a big problem, which it solved by creating a dual carriageway through the middle of the town, and a new set of problems!

The town's cattle mart was located off Panmure Street. People recall moments when animals escaped and rampaged through streets, so although it may not have been an ideal location, it was sufficiently close to the railway to allow beasts to be transported by train, a feature of most early auction markets. The sign painted on the roof of the building on the right indicates that at the time of this picture the mart was owned and operated by the Montrose Auction Company Ltd. When property was demolished to make way for Burnside Drive, the site occupied by the mart also appears to have been cleared and incorporated into the modern bus station. The old bus stance at Brothock Bridge was made unusable when one side of the area was cut off by the new road.

The Victoria Café was situated on Millgate at the point where it crossed the tracks of the branch line that ran between the main railway line and the harbour. The business catered for more things than might be associated with a simple café. There was a commodious hall and rooms for wedding parties, social events, presentations, club meetings and society gatherings, and there was a room set aside for ladies. It offered breakfasts, dinners, teas and suppers, and purveys for picnics and soirees, and all 'at most moderate charges'. Motoring was in its infancy when this picture was used as postcard in 1904, but as the sign on the gable makes clear, the Victoria Café had already moved quickly to attract new car-borne customers.

A few years after 1906 when this picture was used as a postcard, butcher D. Y. Walker was inviting customers to his shop, on the corner of Millgate Loan and West Grimsby, to try his sausages, claiming they were delicious, far famed, and had won many 'golden opinions'. A good buy at nine (old) pence for a pound, as was the three pounds of rinded fat on offer for one shilling and two pence. Every joint of prime beef and other meats was 'very tasty and appetising', and if that wasn't sufficiently tempting, the shop also sold roast, or braised beef, poultry and fresh country eggs. If the thought of all that food made customers thirsty, they could take 'a wee refreshment' at the neighbouring wine and spirit merchant, a business that later expanded to take over the butcher's premises.

Hatter, hosier, glover and tartan specialist, D. R. Macdonald styled his West Port shop as 'The Fit o' the Port' as this picture from the early 1920s shows. He also offered 'Red Lichtie' gentlemen's collars in those days when a shirt would remain clean enough for a few days' wear, but collars got dirty and could be changed, and held in place with a stud. Having got fitted out with caps and collars, men could cross the street to 'The Stag' bar of C. N. Anderson, which stocked 'old scotch whisky' matured in sherry casks. Draught and bottled beer, the best London stouts, brandy, rum, port, and sherry of the highest class were all also on offer to drouthy customers.

The prominent building on the right of this view of Keptie Street was the Imperial Hotel. Erected in the late 19th century it boasted of having superb commercial and coffee rooms, a billiard room and private parlours. In those days, hotel rooms did not normally have en-suite facilities, so the hotel's attractions included bathrooms with hot and cold water. The hotel also offered to have 'boots' attend all trains, to assist guests with their luggage. They didn't have far to go, the building with the arcaded frontage alongside the hotel, in the centre of the picture, was the railway station as it appeared prior to being rebuilt in 1911.

The new railway station of 1911 is seen here with the Imperial Hotel filling the right-hand side of the picture, while two horse-drawn cabs wait on the left for customers. Arbroath got an early taste of train travel with two railway companies, the Arbroath and Forfar, and the Dundee and Arbroath serving the town by the late 1830s. They initially terminated at different stations with a tramway link between them and it was some years before the unified station, with its Keptie Street frontage was built. Being a pioneer in railway development wasn't always best because these companies set their rails five feet, six inches apart on stone blocks, and because that didn't conform to the wooden sleepers and standard gauge adopted by railways elsewhere in the country, all the tracks had to be re-laid.

Early railway companies often had a short life. They promoted and built the lines and usually, but not always, operated services for a while before being absorbed by larger companies. That was certainly true for Arbroath's two early companies, which were both acquired by other owners, which, in turn, were taken over in 1866 by the great Glasgow-based Caledonian Railway. The early railway to the north went around Montrose Basin, but the Edinburgh-based North British Railway Company had ambitions to create a more direct route up the coast with bridges over the Forth, Tay and South Esk. They obtained running powers between Dundee and Arbroath and having successfully bridged the South Esk, opened the line to Montrose in 1881. It placed Arbroath on the new, more direct east coast main line and, as traffic increased, in need of a new station.

Just to the west of the railway station is a kink in Keptie Street known as the Keptie Angle, seen here in an undated picture from the days before motor vehicles ousted horse-drawn carts. In the centre, the house with a flagpole above the door was for a time run as the small Kepties Private Hotel. To the right, a couple of shops occupy a building with the upper floors displaying highly floriferous window boxes. Of these, the one on the right was the Star Pharmacy owned by a James Ruxton who dispensed prescriptions, sold drugs and chemicals, dealt in photographic materials, and in common with most chemists at the time tested people's eyesight and sold spectacles. He lived above the shop and may have been responsible for the window boxes. The neighbouring shop was one of a couple in the town run by bookseller, stationer and newsagent David Bouick.

Just to the west of Keptie Angle is the red sandstone Arbroath West Kirk. Seen here in a picture from the late 1930s, it was erected in the late 1870s as St Margaret's Chapel of Ease, although the distinctive belfry atop the tower was added later. It became a parish church in 1886 and was renamed in 1990 when the congregation united with Ladyloan St Columba's. Opposite the church, but out of view, Arbroath High School was erected in the late 1890s to replace the earlier Academy on Hill Terrace. Also since superseded by a new Arbroath Academy, it has become the further education Angus College. Like the kirk and school, McLean's garage on the left has also seen a few changes of name and ownership.

Situated to the north of Keptie Street, Elliot Street is seen here with a group of residents attracted outside by the presence of the photographer and a delivery van. It belonged to George Salmond, whose bakery at 199 High Street was started in 1867 and, since the picture was used as a postcard in 1911, his claim to have been in business for over 40 years was correct. As well as claiming longevity, Salmond extolled the virtues of his products including his famed Scotch shortbread, 'for quality it excels', 'Fairport Gingerbread' and oatcakes made 'from the finest oats grown on the Braes of Angus'. Whether horse-drawn like this one or motorised as they were later, delivery vans like this were common, serving outlying streets and more distant communities

Picture postcards were very popular in the years before the First World War. Photographers and publishers produced a vast array of cards to meet the high demand, including some depicting unfashionable streets away from town centres. These are valuable social history records because they were not produced in large numbers, but instead sought to attract customers from the neighbourhood by featuring local residents. This picture of Cairnie Street is typical and a customer did buy it, but was unimpressed, describing it in a message as 'not very clear' (they were right), although they did indicate that the card was 'new' and helpfully added the date, 1912. Despite the lack of clarity, the sender thought the recipient would recognise the woman flanked by children standing in the middle of the road.

Heading north from Cairnie Street, St Vigeans Road is shown here in a picture also dated 1912, a time when this distinctive range of tenement dwellings was on the edge of the town. It is typical of late 19th century industrial housing in cities like Dundee and a reminder that Arbroath was, despite its coastal and rural setting, an industrial town. Large power loom factories made linen, with sailcloth a principal product. The industry developed in Scotland through the 18th century and as it expanded the supply of home-grown flax proved insufficient to meet demand and so large quantities had to be imported from the Baltic countries and Germany. The most convenient harbours to land these cargoes were on the east coast, which helped to make Angus generally, and Arbroath in particular, a major centre for the industry.

Situated to the north of Arbroath, the village of St Vigeans has, over time, become part of the larger town. It is seen here with the Brothock Water in the foreground and the parish church standing proudly on its elevated knoll. It's an ancient religious site. Early records suggest a 12th century date for a church consecrated in the mid thirteenth. Altered in the 15th century the present church was remodelled in 1871-72 by the architect R. Rowand Anderson. During that reconstruction work many fragments of Pictish carved stones were discovered, suggesting that the religious significance of the site is older than the church itself. The stones, which include the Drosten Stone with a very rare written inscription, represent a treasure of national importance and have since been housed in an adjacent museum.

Letham Grange, a mansion to the north of St Vigeans, was designed by Aberdeen-born architect Archibald Simpson and built around 1827-30 for John Hay who had inherited the estate assembled by his father Alexander Hay, former Provost of Arbroath. John Hay was unmarried and, with no children to inherit, the estate was sold in 1877 following his death. The new owner altered and enlarged the building, so that its style was as much Victorian as Georgian when it was converted in the 1980s for a new role as a hotel. Golf courses were laid out around it, the 'Old Course', opened in 1987 by Sir Henry Cotton, and the 'New' or 'Glens' course opened in 1992. By 2019 the hotel was shut, the building abandoned and the golf courses closed.

The parish of St Vigeans included Colliston village, located about three miles from Arbroath beside the Brechin road. Traffic has increased markedly in modern times, but when this picture was taken about 1910 the road was evidently much quieter. The carter appears to have halted to deliver supplies to the little shop and post office on the left. Despite its size Colliston could also boast of having that other village essential, an inn, which at about the same time this photograph was taken, was run by Alexander Nairn. A short hop across the fields is Colliston Castle, a mid 16th structure with later modifications associated with Cardinal Beaton and the Guthrie family. Like the traffic on the main road, its role has changed in modern times, to holiday accommodation.

Arbirlot, to the west of Arbroath, is seen here in a view from the bridge over the Elliot Water – the village name is thought to be a corruption of Aberelliot. On the right is the parish church, which was built in 1832 with accommodation for over 600 worshippers, but when the great Disruption of 1843 split the Church of Scotland many parishioners left to join the new Free Church. Lord Panmure, in common with many landowners, opposed the new church and so the appropriately-named minister, Mr Kirk, had to preach in a barn and often, because he had so many adherents, in the neighbouring field. A new Free Church, designed by the architect John Milne, was built in 1854; its gable can just be seen on the left-hand edge of the picture. It became the church hall following the general reunion in 1929.

Lying beside the railway line along the sea shore to the south of Elliot Water is the Arbroath Golf Course, a traditional links laid out by a trio of Fife's finest course designers. Old Tom Morris from St Andrews started the process in 1877 followed in 1907 by Willie Fernie, also from St Andrews, and in 1931 James Braid from Elie carried out further design improvements. It really doesn't get much better than an impressive pedigree like that. Coastal dunes, wind off the sea, three burns running across the course and a scattering of trees, combined with deceptively undulating fairways and greens guarded by over 70 bunkers make this a testing challenge. The Arbroath Golf Club clubhouse and first tee are seen in this picture from the late 1920s. There was also a second clubhouse for the Artisan Golf Club nearby.

The Dundee road has become a lot busier since this picture was taken in the early 1920s with a boy wandering across it and a girl struggling along with a bicycle. She may have got it from the little 'Cycle Depot' in the shed beside the old toll house. Such houses were set up beside turnpike roads, which were built by private companies authorised by parliament to make roads and charge tolls for their use. They were abolished in 1879. Behind the toll house is the infirmary, erected in 1916 on a site donated by the town council. It had a splendid outlook over the sea to the south and south-west, ideal for the health-giving properties of fresh air and sunshine much favoured by the medical profession of the time. In the days before the establishment of the National Health Service in 1948 local hospitals like this were paid for by public subscription and fund-raising.

Like a medieval fortress atop a commanding summit, the town's water tower was erected on Keptie Hill in 1885 to provide the expanding community with a reliable water supply following a drought some years earlier. It was designed by Friockheim-based architect William Gillespie Lamond and built by unemployed men in an early work for welfare scheme. It held 200,000 gallons of water in three separate tanks, drawing the water from a natural spring. It was a typical arrangement for the period, but the times were changing and after only 23 years the tower was superseded by a gravity system that fed water down to the town from a reservoir on the Noran Water in Glenogil.

Two caravan sites were situated to the west of the town, one at Elliot, which offered prompt, personal attention, touring and living vans and a fully stocked general store. The other site, shown here, was adjacent to the Red Lion Service Station on the Dundee Road. It was established in the early 1950s by the service station proprietor on ground adjacent to his premises. In the planning application he also proposed a car park, garage, tearoom, cooking and toilet facilities, and there would be moveable caravans for hire and space for touring vans. The site was clearly enjoyed by the person who sent this picture postcard in 1957 with a message: 'Have had a wonderful holiday here. It's a grand place for the children, lots of amusements. Going to the circus this afternoon'. From those early beginnings, the caravan parks have added many modern facilities and bigger vans.

With the railway on one side and the seashore on the other the parkland of the West Links was always a popular recreation space. For some it offered a bracing walk beside the sea, others could indulge in more energetic sporting activity like tennis or football and those in between could enjoy a gentle round of the putting green, one of the Links' oldest attractions. It is seen here in a picture from 1923 well patronised by all sorts of people, while for some, putting seems to have been a spectator sport. A giant draughts board was also situated close to the putting green as Arbroath enhanced its range of visitor attractions. Surmounting the high common in the background is a reminder of recent less-happy events, the town's war memorial unveiled by Lord Inchcape in June 1922.

There were a number of opportunities along the West Links for people of all ages to dip a toe or more in the water. There was of course the beach and for those hardy souls prepared to brave the cold North Sea, a bathing pavilion with a columned portico provided a place to get ready. For children, the salt-water paddling pool shown in this picture was an ideal facility. It allowed them to splash about safely or sail the little yachts that were a must-have for children visiting the seaside. And while the wee ones played, indulgent adults could sit on the benches and watch, and perhaps snooze. The building seen behind the paddling pool was the open air bathing pool, regarded as the finest such facility in Scotland although its distinctive green and white façade cannot be fully appreciated in a black and white picture.

Ceremonially opened on 7th July 1934 by the Earl of Strathmore, the new filtered salt-water pool was the culmination of Arbroath's bold attempt to reinvent itself as a holiday destination. People flocked to the opening event and were entertained by Bernard Ash and his popular band from 'The Follies', gramophone music was broadcast over the loud speakers and models showed off clothing for the sun. A swimming gala with competitive and novelty races was held, champion divers plunged gracefully from the high boards and Scotland's greatest pre-war swimmer, Ellen King, who had won two silver medals at the Amsterdam Olympic Games in 1928, demonstrated her prowess. The weather could have been kinder, but it was quite a day, after which the pool settled into its role as a prime attraction with facilities like the giant wheel, raft and chute, heated dressing rooms and cafeteria.

Perhaps the most significant of sporting facilities along the sea front to the west of the town is Gayfield Park, the home ground of Arbroath Football Club. Formed in 1878, the club is also known by its nickname, the 'Red Lichties' derived from the red light that guided fishing boats back into harbour. Throughout its history the club has enjoyed many good results, endured a few poor ones and almost scaled the heights to the top division in season 2021-22. Arbroath FC does however hold a record that is unlikely to be equalled; in 1885 the club beat Aberdeen Bon Accord 36-0 in a Scottish cup game, the highest ever score in professional football. Local rivalry has always been fierce with games, especially against Montrose, keenly contested. This team was photographed in the wake of winning the Forfarshire Cup for the season 1913-14 by beating Dundee Hibs.

Football is usually regarded as Scotland's national game and cricket often disparaged, but for many years before football's ascendancy sport was a summer activity and cricket a widely popular game. This certainly seems to have been the case in Arbroath where early clubs amalgamated in 1846 as Arbroath United Cricket Club. In those days it was never easy to find a suitable ground, although a pitch on the Western Common beside the Dundee Road was levelled and turfed. It proved to be less than ideal and so the club moved to a new field at Lochlands. Again the ground had to be levelled and turfed, and with the addition of a pavilion was ready in May 1887 for the official opening match against Perthshire Cricket Club. It was a draw. This team was photographed in 1902.

A drifter that has nosed up to the beach in the outer harbour occupies the foreground of this picture from about 1940 with, behind it, the shore station and signal tower for the Bell Rock lighthouse. The rock, lying about twelve miles off Arbroath, was infamous as a danger to shipping until civil engineer Robert Stevenson erected a lighthouse on it. Work to prepare foundations began in 1807, but it was no easy job. The rock was submerged at high tide and work could only be done for a few hours at a time in the better months, and not even then if the weather was rough. Stevenson devised a system of interlocking stones, which were prepared on shore and shipped out to the construction site. A masons yard for this work was set up along with barracks to accommodate the men and, following completion of the lighthouse, this yard became the site for the shore station and signal tower. Following automation of the light in 1988, the building was turned into a museum.

The harbour was of major importance to Arbroath, providing a safe haven for many vessels including fishing boats like the *Ebenezer*. A local boat, registered AH46, she is seen here in a splendid picture used as a postcard in 1911 with a caption that describes her as a 'motor fishing boat'. Despite that, she appears to be fully set up as a type of east coast sailing drifter known as a 'Fifie'. Such craft were at a disadvantage if trying to get their catch back to harbour in windless conditions and although the development of 'motor' marine engines was in its infancy at this time, having one aboard would be very helpful. Developed on Scotland's east coast after the 1860s, 'Fifies' were typically just short of 80 feet long, fully decked, and with an upright stem and stern. They had two masts, a main and mizzen, and under full sail their long keel made them fast, but conversely they could be slow to answer the helm, which may have been another reason for having a motor.

People have fished out of Arbroath for centuries. In the early days much of this was done using baited lines to catch demersal, bottom feeding fish like haddock, cod or ling, but in the late 18th century the popularity of herring suddenly soared. It's not that this little fish was unknown, Dutch and other Continental fishermen had been scooping up the shoals of the silver darlings for a long time, but when British people realised they were missing out on a nutritious fish, and a lucrative export market, a major industry was born. The people who worked in it tended to be itinerant with the boats and shore-based activities moving around the coasts from the Outer Hebrides to the East Coast. For a long time people thought they were following migrating shoals of herring, but later the industry realised that separate shoals turned up in different locations as the season progressed.

The splendid pictures on these two pages convey a sense of the busy activity generated by the industry. The boats have delivered the fish and the 'fisher lassies', as they were known, who worked at great speed, have gutted them and are packing them into barrels. Some coopers on the left of the picture on the facing page appear to be closing barrel tops with a final hoop. To get the government seal of approval, barrels had to be tightly packed along with salt to preserve the fish in a briny solution. The man standing on the barrels in the background here appears to using his own weight to finish the job. Such was the volume of fish processed by the industry that in less than a hundred years the herring boom was over, and boats working out of harbours like Arbroath could return to more sustainable activities.

Arbroath Harbour consists of a tidal basin and a wet dock. The dock was originally made in the 18th century as a tidal basin, but was reconstructed in 1839 by engineer James Leslie whose designs also included the building of the outer tidal harbour. The wet dock was fully enclosed in the 1870s, with gates to fix the water level. It is seen here in the 1930s occupied by a couple of small coasters. A branch railway that ran down through the town connected the harbour with the main line and provided transport for the cargoes shipped in and out on vessels like these. Rising above the houses, beyond the Belfast-registered *Tory Island*, are the cooling towers of the electricity works set up on South Grimsby by the Arbroath Electric Light and Power Company.

That other essential civic utility in the late 19th and early 20th century, a gas works, was located off Ponderlaw Street and is seen in the background to this picture of Springfield Park, to the east of the harbour. Created out of a small estate acquired by the town council, this was very different to the open links west of the town. Springfield was a traditional town park where people could listen to music at the bandstand, relax in the tranquillity of floral gardens or take to the putting greens. There was also a children's play park and the facility being used by a little girl in the centre of this picture, a drinking fountain. Such things were common in public places in the late 1950s when this picture was taken, but have since been removed as possible health hazards. All traces of the prehistoric stone cist burials discovered on the eastern side of the park have also disappeared.

Adjoining Springfield Park is Victoria Park, a wide-open area marching along the shoreline. Opened in 1897 to commemorate Queen Victoria's Diamond Jubilee, it is a natural amphitheatre, event space and place for open-air markets. It is also blessed with stunning views that entice the inquisitive to venture further to see the dramatic coastal cliff scenery to the north. These walkers were photographed in 1923 crossing the bridge leading from the park to Whiting Ness, the Steeple Rock and the formation known as the Horse Shoe. Beyond these splendid features are the Needle E'e, a natural rock arch, The Blowhole, Seaton Cliffs Nature Reserve, the delightful Seaton Den and more caves, coves, bays and headlands before the little village of Auchmithie is reached.

At Auchmithie the great red cliffs recede just enough to form a small sheltered cove, which some indomitable people regarded as a good place to keep a small boat and go fishing on the daunting North Sea. Initially there was no harbour and the boats had to be hauled up onto the beach after every trip, and of course launched with some effort before going to sea. A harbour wall was built about 1890, but within ten years it had to be repaired after storm damage. It can be seen on the right of this picture, which although undated appears to be from about 1910. A cluster of boats rests on the beach while high above, atop the cliffs, is the village. Auchmithie folk must have been fit as well as tough having regularly to climb the steep slope to and from the beach.

Auchmithie acted as a magnet for early photographers, as pictures like this show. Other artists were also attracted to the village; Sir Walter Scott based scenes and characters in his novel *The Antiquary* on the village, and the Newtyle-born painter, William Bradley Lamond, (1857-1924) moved there during many summer seasons while he painted the wild coast and seascapes. This artistic activity may have amused the villagers, but they still had to make a living. They did this by line fishing, using strings of baited hooks and it was usually the women who sat for hours baiting the hooks. Eventually the laborious use of the beach ended in favour of working boats out of Arbroath Harbour, but the villagers can claim one lasting legacy; they originated the famous 'Arbroath smokie' – salted haddock suspended over a half-barrel of burning wood chips and covered with a wet cloth to keep in the smoke – delicious!